Work For You

Join the Internet Marketing Revolution

Jim Stephens

"Tips On How To Secretly Create An Online Income Stream While Working 9-5 – And Go Full Time Before You Know It!"

TABLE OF CONTENTS

"Tips On How To Secretly Create An Online Income Stream While Working 9-5 – And Go Full Time Before You Know It!"

Chapter 1: Introduction

Welcome to Fire Your Boss And Join The Internet Marketing Revolution!

Most people would like to start a home business. They like the freedom of being able to work whenever they want to or wherever they want to. However, it is not easy to get there because many of them are stuck in a rut!

They feel that they are controlled by their bosses. They feel that it would take too much time.

Some of them even whine that they are too tired to do anything the moment they reach home!

Whatever your excuses may be, you will most probably find the solution in this book (or at least, know what it takes to get started). The fact that you are able to pick up this book and read it shows your initiative and you should congratulate yourself for taking the first step!

The Internet is a place that is filled with endless possibilities. It is very easy to find a business model that makes money for anyone as long as they put in the effort to learn and work hard.

All that it takes is that you believe in yourself and believe that you will be able to free yourself from the shackles of your 9-5 job and you will be able to find the means to achieve it.

After all, if you want something badly enough, you will go all out and find the means to achieve your goals.

Alright! Let's get started immediately!

Chapter 2: Key Concepts behind This Book

In this book, you will learn all about the following:

- The type of mentality one must adopt if they ever want to break out from the rat race!
- How to turn your skills into your greatest assets!
- How to pick a business model and apply your skills to it!
- How to invest merely 4 hours a day and be able to quit your job or fire your boss... within 6 months!
- Lots of resources to get you started IMMEDIATELY!

Working Part Time with A Full Time Mentality

One of the biggest reasons why people fail at Internet marketing (or fail to break out of their rat race) is because of a flawed mindset towards Internet marketing.

Yes, it is true that you have to spend the remainder of the hours you have left after work to work on your business part time. But that does NOT mean that you will adopt a part time or half-hearted mentality towards your business.

Imagine this analogy...

Let's assume that an airplane takes off at 150MPH. You will need to 'drive' at a certain speed before the plane develops enough speed to take off. Do you think the plane will be able to fly itself off the ground if you are only traveling at a 100MPH? Of course not! It will not take off even if you are flying at 140MPH!

Internet marketing is just like this. You will need to work at a certain momentum before you:

- Develop the necessary knowledge to build your business (you can't really 'drive' far if you are constantly locked in 2nd gear).

- You need to show others that you are committed enough before they are ready to do a joint venture with you (after all, no one wants to JV with a half-hearted marketer – especially if they know that you are not constantly available).

- You need to build your reputation strong enough because it will lessen your promotion work – the speed of trust between you and your customers is very crucial.

The Art of Building Assets Online

When you are building your business online, you must be able to build assets if you want to quit your job. Allow me to explain:

A 9-5 job is only short term income. It can be a lot or a little, but fundamentally it is still short term... Why? Because the moment you stop working, you stop making money immediately!

Your boss may tolerate your laziness for a few days but if you don't put in the hours, you will never get anymore pay whether it is weekly, daily or monthly pay!

If you keep on trading time for money, you will never be free from your job!

Online assets are different. Here are a few principles that you can apply to your online mentality:

- **Leveraging on the Internet**: You can draw in traffic from search engines or viral marketing.

- **Leveraging on other Internet marketers**. You do not need to build a mailing list if you have created a fantastic product that will keep customers buying and affiliates selling over and over again.

- **Leveraging on your mailing list**. The money is definitely in the list. It takes 15-30 minutes to write a proper E-mail to your mailing list. The great thing about E-mail marketing is you will take the same time to mail your list regardless if your list has 100 people or 100,000 people

- **Leveraging on your reputation online**: A blogger may start with no RSS subscribers, but the more you blog and the more you network, you will be blogging for the same effort but with more people reading your blog (and you will be able to monetize from the traffic!)

- **Leveraging on outsourced work**. If you are making good money, you will be able to outsource your work to other people and spend more time on marketing your products (hence, making more money!)

Take a look at this graph for example:

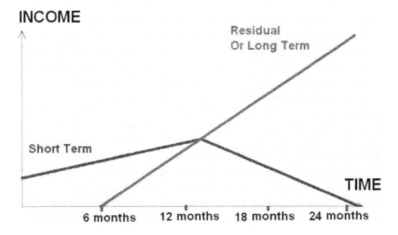

Let's take a look at a typical Internet Marketer…

The blue line is your 9-5 job. You may get increments and bonuses (hence the rising graph and your salary will most definitely exceed your online income in the first few months, but after awhile, when your online assets start generating residual income, you will be able to quit your job once you have all the elements in place.

Investing Into Your Assets through Outsourcing

Not everyone can do everything at once. Even if you are proficient at all the tasks (albeit a master of none...), you will still need to outsource from time to time as the need to create more and more assets should NOT be limited by your time alone but by creating more through leveraging on other people's time.

Remember this principle; the sum of the whole is more than the parts combined.

You may outsource certain tasks like writing, graphics or SEO services, but ultimately you must develop a goal (using a proven business model) that will piece everything together and synergize.

In the next chapter, we will explore a little on core competencies which is also related to outsourcing in general.

Chapter 3: Monetizing Your Core Competencies

The best way to start your business off the right foot is to examine yourself and see what your best skills are. Here is a list of which business model you are able to excel with:

- Writing
- Graphics Design
- Statistics
- Programming
- Networking

Monetizing Your Writing Skills

A writer is always in demand amongst Internet marketing circles. You will be able to monetize in the areas of ghostwriting, copywriting, blogging, article writing, newsletter publishing and content creation.

Contrary to what some people may assume, creating a written product is one of the most daunting tasks a person can undertake. Unless you have a flair for writing, nobody in their right mind will mass produce E-books (unless they are willing to make huge sacrifices for their financial goals).

Writers are also a great asset when it comes to product launches in Internet marketing. You will be able to find joint venture partners easily if you are willing to contribute your writing skills to the areas of writing sales letters, E-courses, and promo E-mails.

Recommended Resources

If You Are Looking For Ways to Monetize Your Writing Skills Easily, Check Out This Free Guide (Worth $37) On How To Make Money Online With Writing

Monetizing Your Graphics Designing Skills

Graphic designers are also very important within the Internet marketing niche. A graphic designer can easily earn a hundred dollars for good quality E-covers, blog banners and site graphics.

You can even sell the Photoshop PSD file by giving away the rights for someone to rebrand them on their own sites.

One of the reasons why a graphic designer (or artist) is always in demand is because graphics tend to sell themselves.

People DO judge a book by its cover and it is very important to tap into this psychological factor. It can make the difference between getting a sale and NOT getting a sale.

Recommended Resources

If You Want More Information on How To Monetize
Graphics Then Get The Latest News Here

Analyzing Statistics

As surprising as it may sound, making money online is all about analyzing statistics. You can learn a lot from analyzing data such as your click through rates (how many people click on your links or your ads), your impressions (how times you page or ads are loaded) and your conversion rates – how much money you make each time someone visits your website!

You will be able to track your statistics properly using the following tools – Google Analytics and Statcounter . Sign up here for a free account and instructions on how to use these tools.

Programming

If you are good at programming, you will be able to excel when it comes to installing scripts like The butterfly marketing script , JV Manager and many others that require technical skills.

HTML and PHP skills also come in handy when it comes to blogging and other web based software.

Networking

This skill is quite valuable when it comes to finding JV partners and outsourcing.

Just like in the real world, networking is also equally important when it comes to building friendships and getting people to promote your products.

If you want to excel in Internet marketing, you must not sit in front of your computer without talking to anyone. A person who is good at networking offline is also able to do the same online – it is just that the medium that is used is different (using MSN or SKYPE or Yahoo! Messenger).

You can also go to World Internet Summits (WIS) or other Internet marketing conventions to touch base with other marketers and speakers.

Recommended Resources

This Is The Most Popular Forum On The Internet When It Comes To Internet Marketing. Get To Know Lots Of People And Build Networks/Relationships at The Warrior Forum!

Chapter 4: Choosing the Right Models

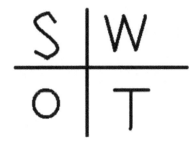

(Diagram Of SWOT Analysis – Strengths, Weaknesses, Opportunities, Threats)

Here are some tips on what opportunities may be suitable for you and how you can strategize your way to build your income online so that you will be able to quit your job.

Blogging

Blogging is one of the easiest models that someone can attempt. Almost anyone can become a blogger. Even those who can't write (picture blogs).

Strengths: You can blog about anything you want! Focus on your passion and share your thoughts with the world. If you have great content, people will come to your blog and you can monetize through advertising or affiliate programs. The startup cost is only $9 and it costs about $5 a month to maintain this business model (You only pay for the domain name and monthly hosting respectively.) You can even register some blogs for free!

Weaknesses: It may take a long time to build up traffic – an average person who blogs regularly but slowly may quit his or her job within one to two years. If you want to achieve freedom in half the time, you have to blog and network with other bloggers more aggressively.

Opportunities: You may not be able to see yourself making money at the start, but to offset that, you can blog for others (for a fee) or even sign up for PAY PER POST and get paid for blogging!

Threats: There is a blog born or created every **TWO SECONDS**. So you can imagine how much competition you are going up against!

Suggested Course Of Action: Register a personal domain name now! This is very important because the most important person in the world is YOU and getting a domain after your own name is the most important thing you must do. Then you can start blogging about yourself.

Affiliate Marketing

Affiliate marketing is one of the most lucrative models on the Internet. You can promote other people's product and get commissions for your efforts without seeing a single customer or talking to anyone.

Strengths: You don't even need a domain name or a website in some cases. You can earn huge commissions from up to 50% to even 100% commissions! You don't need to focus on creating products – just drive traffic to the merchant site and watch your income roll in (if you do it right of course).

Weaknesses: You will need to search for a good affiliate program and build up traffic in order to see results.

Opportunities: There are unlimited opportunities because there are always new products coming out each day and affiliates are needed everywhere!

Threats: You are competing against THOUSANDS of affiliates out there and those affiliates are your competitors. Some programs even offer two-tier programs and established affiliates probably have dozens of affiliates under them as well.

Suggested Course Of Action: Register as an affiliate at Commission Junction , Clickbank or Amazon . Find good products to promote – especially those with good 'gravity'.

Online Network Marketing

If network marketing is your cup of tea, then you must learn to explore new opportunities by promoting network marketing programs on the Internet.

Strengths: Similar to affiliate marketing, you don't need to see anybody and promote your programs online. You have the entire world's Internet users as your prospects for your downline groups.

Weaknesses: Building a network marketing business online is prone to being impersonal. Make sure you do not adopt a 'build and burn' mentality.

Opportunities: You can easily recruit more people online compared to doing something offline (where you are limited by time and space)

Threats: Globalization – downlines are not as loyal as they used to be due to the abundance of opportunities available on the Internet.

Suggested Course Of Action: Sign up for a network marketing prospecting system that will help you to generate lots of fresh leads while making money at the same time.

Niche Marketing

Niche marketing is a term people use to refer to niches that people can target to make money online without focusing on 'business opportunity' or 'make money' niches (like Internet marketing or network marketing).

It targets niches such as self-improvement, dog training, gaming, movies or other things that do not fall into the category of money making niches.

Strengths: You can focus on your passion and become an expert in it. Let's say you are an expert at mountain biking, then talk all about it and monetize from this niche alone.

Weaknesses: You have to be plan everything and make sure your traffic is quite targeted and an expert at it. Different niches yield different results.

Opportunities: Niche marketing opportunities are ENDLESS. All you need to do is find a niche you can excel in that nobody else is targeting (of course, this is very rare but a lot of niches are not that congested).

Threats: An untapped niche is rare – so most people go for rarer sub-niches

Suggested Course Of Action: Do a search on Google for "YOUR NICHE" FORUM (Example: if you are targeting the gaming niche, type in "gaming forum") this will be your market!

Freelance Services

The fastest way to make money online – offer your services as a freelancer based on your core competencies and earn money immediately by cashing in on your expertise!

Strengths: Fast and good money if you have the right clientele. In fact, this is one of the fastest ways to quit your full time job – just become a freelancer and be the boss of your own time!

Weaknesses: You need to have a skill and market your services. You have to build up your clientele as well and have them recommend more business to you.

Opportunities: Writers, graphic designers and other talents are in demand especially on the Internet.

Threats: You are competing against other freelancers, many of them sell their services TOO CHEAP!

Suggested Course Of Action: Go to E-lance and look for work there.

Internet Marketing

The most popular niche online – mostly related to teaching others how to make money online or business opportunity niches.

Strengths: There is a huge hungry market here looking to find the holy grail of making money online. If you have a product that can help them to make money, save money, save time, save effort or generally run their business for them, then you have a huge market here.

Weaknesses: This is one niche that you must make sure you produce results for your prospects. Don't be a hypocrite by telling others you can teach them to make money online but you haven't made a single cent!

Opportunities: There are lots of niches like resell rights, private label rights, product creation, search engine optimization and many more – you just need to find which market you are more comfortable with.

Threats: This is the MOST COMPETITIVE niche online – everyone is fighting for the same pie – but people are also willing to buy...

Suggested Course Of Action: Go to Make Your Living Online and learn all about it.

Chapter 5: Work 4 Hours A Day and Retire In 6 Months

Now that you have discovered a few business models you can work with, you must get started immediately! Take action right now!

Here are a few tips that will assist you and help you to achieve your goals within 6 months!

Think long term

Do not just think of earning 'enough'. You need to think long term and build a business that is sustainable.

It is like shooting for the stars. If you shoot for the stars, you might not be able to clear the skies, but at least, you will be able to cross the fence.

If you aim too low or too short term, you will fail easily because more than often, we usually don't usually accomplish our goals to our expectations.

Build your business around your interests

In some business models like blogging, you must be passionate about what you are doing.

If you do not build your business around your interests, people will be able to sense it. It would look 'fake' and you will not be able to sustain your interests. Before long, you will be thinking about giving up.

If your business if focused on your interests, you will not feel as though you are taking another job. After all, having ONE job is already bad enough. We want to FREE ourselves from our job, not get another one.

Invest your salary into your business

Certain business models require you to make some investments. Like outsourcing, buying domain names, paid traffic and others. Do not believe the myth that it doesn't cost money to build a business online – it is inexpensive but NOT free.

The advantage of having a job is that you can invest some of your salary to get things done. After all you only have 4 hours and the weekends to build your business. You must learn to invest your time AND money wisely to achieve maximum results.

Putting up with negative people

The idea of making money online is a foreign concept to many people. If you tell them that you want to quit your job within 6 months, they will look at you with a strange look in their eyes.

In some cases, they will try and discourage you, so you must have very clear goals otherwise; you will never be able to quit your job within 6 months (or in some cases – 2 years). You don't want people to laugh at you if you don't reach your 6 month goal so you must succeed AT ALL COSTS!

Chapter 6: Recommended Resources for Fast Startup

Now that you have learned the mindset, found the best model and allocated time to work on your business, it's time to jumpstart your business IMMEDIATELY!

If you want to skyrocket your own businesses as quickly as possible, here are some resources that you can check out to help you get started as without getting into too much hassle:

Ready Niche Business

Gain access to a turnkey system of ready made products – from E-books, special reports, sales letters, squeeze pages, E-course, articles, blog posts and niche research all done and ready to be monetized.

Resell Rights Mastery

You can get free resources here at Resell Rights Mastery. Tons of E-books, software, reports and articles all ready to help you start your business.

Private Label Rights Products

This is one of the most comprehensive private label rights membership sites has all the content you will need to get started with. You will not need to write a single word for an entire year.

SEO Services

Alfred Ko is known as the **'Aggressive SEO Guy'**. His services are designed to get your sites up on the first page on Google using aggressive SEO techniques .

Graphics Design

Rapid Fire Studio is another good graphics design site that you can use to get good quality graphics produced for your E-covers if designing graphics is not your core competency.

List Building Tools

List building on steroids. This is one of the newest and most important software applications available on the Internet.

You can use it to build a huge mailing list. One guy even used it to generate over 1,200 subscribers in 5 days.

Check out how it works here .

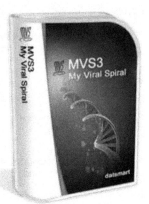

Chapter 7: Summary

The most important thing you must remember is to break through your mental barriers. The only thing that is holding us back is ourselves.

I told my friend to go and start a site. He told me that it is a great idea and he will start it SOMEDAY (while saying that his job stinks!)

He never took action, and today he is still stuck in his rut saying that 'someday' he will start his site…

Be serious about your dreams and your goals.

Treat Your Internet Business As A Real Business And You Will Be Able To Fire Your Boss IN NO TIME!

To your Success!

www.ingramcontent.com/pod-product-compliance
Lightning Source LLC
Chambersburg PA
CBHW052143070326
40690CB00047B/2052